THE SIGNIFICANCE OF

SUSTAIN ABILITY

KYLE Z. MICHAUD

Kyle Z. Michaud Publications

DEDICATION

For our children's children

Table of Contents

INTRODUCTION

"Glance at the sun
See the moon and the stars
Gaze at the beauty of the earth's greenings.
Now, think."

—Hildegard von Bingen

The word "sustainability" has become a cornerstone of the everyday vocabulary of millions of people all around the globe. For many, it is considered to be the word of the century, or even millennium. Interestingly, it has been used in a variety of ways, with an array of meanings. In 1992, at the Earth Summit in Rio de Janeiro sponsored by the United Nations, the word "sustainable development" was used for the first time, specifically in the context of a 1987 report entitled, "Our Common Future." The term "sustainable development" was here defined as: "development that meets the needs of the present without compromising the ability of future generations to meet their own needs."

Although this quote is vague in defining the factors that could potentially have a negative impact on the survival of future generations, the definition gives humanity something to think about, along with the motivation to find ways to effectively rescue the planet for the future of mankind. Since this declaration at Earth Summit, there's an ongoing mission to educate the world about impending dangers that threaten our future.

Simple daily tasks that seem innocent pile up toward our inevitable destruction. There has been some success along the way in various countries as their top corporate houses have agreed to lend their complete support to this cause, as well as forming their own initiatives to spread the message.

We share the same earth, air, water, and heat with every other organism on this planet.

The greatest challenge in spreading the word on sustainability is educating individuals on the steps they must take to help save the planet. A majority of the blame can be traced to the way the message surrounding sustainability has been propagated throughout the world.

During the initial years of its discussion, the most common images used to represent the subject of our deteriorating world were often oil wells and smoking factory chimneys. Large corporations have often been blamed for their greed and its repercussions like global warming and climate change.

For a while, many of us were satisfied with this half-truth as it was presented to us. Seldom did we have the courage to look into our own lives and our own homes to determine the impact our habits have on our immediate environments.

Being that we are the most dominant and ecologically advanced species on the planet, it is our responsibility to realize how much goodness we can contribute to help save this beautiful world for our children, and our children's children; after all, we all share the same Earth, air, water, and heat. Thus far, our ignorance has played a huge role in alienating us from our natural surroundings, reducing our ability to effectively put an end to all destructive activities.

As bleak as this sounds, luckily it is not too late to make a change. We might just have enough time to be made aware of our mistakes, and to attempt to rectify them by making the necessary changes in our daily lives. We begin this process by diving back into our natural-born connection with nature – a connection that has been missing for centuries.

This writing serves an important purpose to help everyone understand sustainability in its true importance in the role of supporting and nurturing future generations. Making the correct decisions in our everyday lives will lead to a plethora of natural resources for our children, and our children's children.

CHAPTER ONE

UNDERSTANDING SUSTAINABILITY

"Sustainability, ensuring the future of life on Earth, is an infinite game, the endless expression of generosity on behalf of all."

—Paul Hawken

To ensure the success of sustainable development, we must first begin at home with our own health and lifestyle choices. Consistently encouraging better lifestyle choices for our children will create a culture of sustainability passed down through the years, eventually becoming the norm in society.

Research[1] proves that if we want to achieve a sustainable society we must first pursue the following goals:

- Responsible economic growth

- Fair social growth

- Effective environmental protections

These three key elements hold within them the structure

of a sustainable world. The strength they provide will effectively determine the lifespan of our planet. As easy as this may seem to some of us, it has proven to be the biggest challenge to mankind yet.

Sometimes these goals seem impossible to reach. However, if we all work together, momentous changes can ensue. Our movement is comprised of those of us who truly believe that our ultimate survival rests in the hands of attaining a society and environment in a state of sustainability.

SUSTAINABILITY FRAMEWORKS

Since the beginning of time, people have searched for ways to achieve longevity and optimum living conditions for all, as well as alternative ways to help future generations thrive.

Sustainability frameworks provide the method and the tools to effectively achieve sustainability. They support organizations, non-governmental bodies, leaders, and individuals in handling the issues surrounding the goal of sustainability, ultimately providing us with everything we need to get the job done.

With a growing interest in sustainability around the globe, several frameworks target various levels of sustainability. These include: financial, business, and social sustainability—and, so on. Being that we are most concerned with the contributions of individuals to make for a better world, our focus will rest on frameworks that work toward a common goal.

THE NATURAL STEP (TNS)[2]

We came upon this framework when it was given to us by a nonprofit organization in Sweden sharing the same name. The face behind the organization is Karl Henrik Robèrt. This framework states that nature is not subject to systematically increasing:

•   Concentrations of substances extracted from the Earth's crust

•   Concentrations of substances produced by society

• Degradation by physical means, and within that society

• Human needs are not met worldwide

These points focus on interactions between us and the planet and are the basis upon which the following conclusions are drawn:

1. Man mines and procures minerals at a faster pace than they are returned to the Earth's crust

2. Society introduces substances at too fast a rate for them to degenerate through natural forces

3. Humans use natural resources faster than they can regenerate

These conclusions point to the fact that extreme human activity on the Earth can do nothing but bad for the environment, completely negating any chances of complete sustainability. For example, factors such as the combustions of fossil fuels, the constant emission of bio-accumulative chemicals, and the consistent loss of rain forests and wetlands will never make for a sustainable world—in fact, quite the opposite. Additionally, our selfish focus on gaining wealth and good health is destroying a system we heavily rely on – nature.

Further, we are destroying our planet's productive capabilities by polluting both its atmosphere and bodies of water alike. There is no doubt that this depletion and degradation of natural resources will one day come back to bite us. It is like someone passing through a funnel – in the beginning, the funnel provides plenty of space and an abundance of resources, and you enjoy it. After a while, though, you find yourself in a passage that is shrinking. You start wondering about the lost space, searching for ways to widen it. Currently, with the diminishing of natural resources and earth's production capabilities, we are seeking out ways to reverse this funnel. Again, sustainability is the most productive solution.

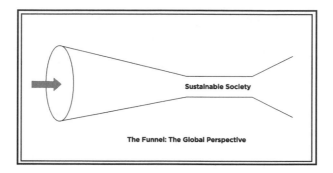

The Funnel: The Global Perspective

That natural step, known as a 5-level framework or 5LF, presents a comprehensive model for planning and decision-making. The five levels include:

- System

- Success

- Strategic

- Actions

- Tools

The five steps allow an individual or organization to create effective strategies for dealing with any present-day situation by incorporating a perspective for a sustainable future.

ECOLOGICAL FOOTPRINT[3]

Ecological Footprint is an organization that uses technology to estimate just how much human demands impact the ecosystem, as well as the amount of space needed by each individual in order to survive. This space includes both productive land and water from which the following human resources are obtained:

- Energy

- Clothing

- Building materials

- Food

- Water

Ecological Footprint's methodology also calculates the amount of space needed to handle the amount of waste produced by each person and individual country. In essence, it measures an ecological footprint.

One of the main factors that influences the aforementioned methodology is human population. It goes without saying that the larger the population, the more a country's consumption increases, and the greater its consequent ecological footprint. As such, countries like the US, China, and India currently have the largest ecological footprints.

How many planets we'd need if everyone lived like a resident of the following:	
Balanced Budget	**Global Deficit**
USA 5 Planets	
UK 3.4	
Argentina 1.7	
South Africa 1.5	
China 1.0	
India 0.4	
World Average 1.4	Credit InfoGrafik.com

Based on current studies, the average ecological footprint per person globally is 2.6 global hectares, or 6.5 global acres. The average allowance per individual is 1.8 global hectares (4.5 global acres). What this means is that to sustain the current population, we need approximately 1.4 earths.

The fact that we are consuming too much is further reflected in the following frightening statistics[4]:

•   Our planet needs at least 18 months to regenerate what we use in 12 months. Our consumption has led to a 44% increase in carbon dioxide, more than nature can provide

•   Within the last 30 years, one-third of the Earth's natural resources have been consumed

•   The US has less than 4% of its original forests

•   40% of the waterways in the US have become undrinkable

•   With 5% of the world's population contained, the US consumes 30% of the world's resources, producing 30% more waste

•   The average US citizen today consumes twice as much as he or she did 50 years ago

As you can see, the repercussions of this very crucial situation are crashing down around us with climate change, shrinking forests, and the loss of biodiversity and water habitats. What's worse is the fact that the fate of our today, tomorrow, and the future of mankind, will be absolutely defined by these limitations on resources.

CHAPTER TWO

HUMAN ACTIVITIES THAT DESTROY THE EARTH

"Here is your country. Cherish these natural wonders, cherish the natural resources, cherish the history and romance as a sacred heritage, for your children and your children's children. Do not let selfish men or greedy interests skin your country of its beauty, its riches or its romance."

—Theodore Roosevelt

When you look at the Earth from out in space, it shines like an absolute gem with its beautiful blues and greens swirling all about. Unfortunately, there are very few in this world who will ever have the opportunity to take in such a view. We do, however, have spectacular photographs from the lenses of both astronauts and satellites alike. It is difficult to look at these photographs without becoming completely mesmerized. Likewise, seeing these photos makes it hard to understand the size of the imprint we are leaving on our beautiful planet.

While humanity has been thriving on Earth for centuries, our most recent activities within the last 100 years have had the most momentous impact on our ecology. Our behavior has become reckless, and the choices we have made in terms of conspicuous consumption are now playing huge roles in the destruction of this once great planet. From high rates of carbon dioxide emissions to diverting almost one-third of the Earth's fresh water to farmlands —we are not on the path toward sustainability or rebuilding.

OVERPOPULATION

One of the more prevalent issues facing our planet today is overpopulation. There has been a steep rise in the population around the globe, quickly widening our carbon footprint. To put it in perspective, if everyone's consumption matched America's, we would need no less than three to five Earths to sustain us all. This figure will only continue to grow in the coming years if we do not dig in deep and put in efforts toward population control.

In recent years, the key factor to overpopulation has not been illiteracy or lack of sex education in public schools. Rather, improved medical facilities have significantly lowered mortality rates. Although this shines a light on a positive side of human advancement, overpopulation remains, nevertheless, a threat to our planet's sustainable development and very existence.

CONSUMERISM

The rising rate of consumerism among developed and developing countries also poses a threat to our ecological balance. Economists may view it as a positive for the world economy, but this rise in consumption produces large levels of waste material. You might be shocked to learn that the scrap industry thrives due to waste materials that are shipped out to other countries that recycle them for future use. However, a lot of waste material fails to reach its destination, ending up scattered, burned, and, well, wasted.

Besides the nauseating smell, burning waste materials releases copious amounts of toxic gas into the atmosphere, affecting both those nearest to the burn sites as well as everybody else around the world.

Below are the factors that have increased the amount of waste materials in landfills.

- Growth of the population

- Waste reduction efforts

75% of the waste generated in a typical residential remodel **can be recycled or reused**

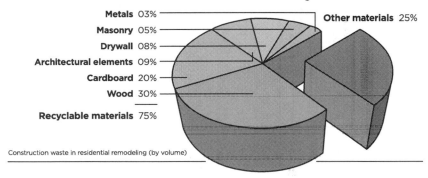

Metals 03%	Other materials 25%
Masonry 05%	
Drywall 08%	
Architectural elements 09%	
Cardboard 20%	
Wood 30%	
Recyclable materials 75%	

Construction waste in residential remodeling (by volume)

Key facts include[5]:

- It is estimated that solid waste will exceed 11 million tons a day by the year 2100

- Municipal solid waste creates 14-20% of all waste generated worldwide, while other waste types include construction and demolition (30%), manufacturing (20%), mining and quarrying (2%)

- A large portion of the waste generated worldwide (57% to 85%) is disposed of in landfills, including open and engineered landfills

- Perhaps most worrying of all is the increase in inorganic and hazardous wastes—318 and 338 million tons generate, respectively, throughout 2000 and 2001

- While the problems involved with consumerism and waste management increase, we must focus heavily on recycling and reusing.

OVERUSE OF RESOURCES

Our lives here on Earth are highly dependent on basic resources like water, forest, soil, and so forth. Throughout the years, we have overused these resources for our personal development and more unnecessarily, for our personal comfort. Recent data shows that because of low amounts of rainfall due to deforestation and man-made dams, one-fourth of all of Earth's river basins are run dry before ever reaching the ocean. A sad fact indeed. Less rainfall, of course, has also resulted in low crop yields and a reduction in the overall animal population in various regions.

Another factor that weighs heavily on the environment is mining. Mining inevitably leads to:

- The destruction of natural landscapes and wildlife habitats

- The destruction of the fertile top layer of soil

- Creating unusable land with the presence of harmful elements unearthed from the depths

- Noise and dust pollution

Unfortunately, the activities mentioned above are not the end of the negative consequences of mining. While attempting to reach the pinnacle of development, we have forgotten about the importance of conserving the very Earth from which we receive our resources.

CHAPTER THREE

SUSTAINABILITY: WHAT IT MEANS TO OUR FUTURE GENERATIONS

"What's the use of a fine house if you haven't got a tolerable planet to put it on?"

—Henry David Thoreau, *Familiar Letters*

Using our planet's precious resources at the rate at which we are secures absolutely no chance at sustainability for future generations—therefore, no real future for them, either. Thus far, we have failed to realize our responsibility to this planet and its conservation, not only for ourselves, but for the future. Lest we forget, the responsibility of caring for Mother Earth does not lie in the hands of the government or some special organizations alone, but in our hands – as citizens of this planet.

Now that we have taken an active look at the true meaning and gravity of sustainable development, we must learn the ways in which we can contribute toward this necessary dream. While it is not necessarily an easy task to take on, it is not rocket science either. Being aware of our individual roles and the impact we have is a must. The choice starts with each one of us, and we must be educated to make the right one.

For sustainable development to manifest, we must:

- Choose to use sustainable products

- Work on energy and carbon savings

- Minimize our waste output

- Actively conserve water

- Design sustainable architecture

- Promote low carbon transportation

CHOOSING SUSTAINABLE PRODUCTS

Choosing sustainable materials and products for personal consumption is the first step toward creating a sustainable world. To decipher between "green," sustainable, and others, you first need to understand a product's entire life cycle.

Many products we have today are manufactured by chains of suppliers. These suppliers process materials or assemble components prior to their final delivery when they are ready for customers. Heavy environmental impacts occur during each stage, from processing, to manufacturing, through transporting.

The most commonly accepted method for life-cycle assessment, or LCA, is defined by the International Standards Organization (ISO14040 and ISO14044). LCA effectively calculates environmental footprints at each stage during the products creation, use, and disposal. The most common things assessed include[6]:

- Embodied energy from non-renewable resources like fossil fuels

- Embodied energy from renewable sources

- The greenhouse potential and analysis of emissions that cause climate change

•   Acidification potential to buildings, vegetation, and ocean life

•   Ozone depletion potential for levels of emissions leading to the thinning of the ozone layer

•   Eutrophication potential for emissions that increase nutrients in the water and soil

•   Photochemical ozone creation potential for emission levels of chemicals that create smog

ENERGY AND CARBON SAVINGS

Consumers today have the ability to research and select the most sustainable products on the market. By doing so we reward the efforts of eco-friendly designers and manufacturers in keeping the planet green.

Being that so many products and brands currently claim green status, how can it be so difficult for consumers to choose the correct products? Currently, many countries require that manufacturers print details of their environmental impact right on the packaging. Packaging is also a good place to look for instructions on whether the product should be recycled at the end of its use.

Some of the more upfront brands even provide the following details:

•   The amount of recycled material used in the manufacturing or packaging process

•   The energy efficiency of the product and/or its carbon footprint

•   An eco-label to help consumers understand how energy efficient and eco-friendly the product is

Amidst the plethora of "green products," there are only a true few that meet specific criteria for being truly eco-friendly. These criteria were determined with great deliberation, bearing life cycles in mind.

These criteria are then translated into design and construction methodologies, including ways to find green materials from their counterparts. Now we need to initiate manufacturing methods that will ensure production of efficient, sustainable products with minimal impact on our Earth.

Effectively manufacturing green, eco-friendly products for the masses will be a bit of a journey. We are growing in our knowledge of how to create better raw materials, thus making results much more real. There is also an increase in consumers who pledge their desire to consume better products that will benefit both them and their environment.

When the green concept was first presented in the mid-twentieth century, it was hard to find any real advocates of the idea. Things have changed as of late, and we are now seeing hundreds of thousands of fierce supporters.

Pro-environment movements are helping us all to understand the real meaning of development. In no way, shape, or form should we allow our greed to compromise our ability to ensure a sustainable future for our children. We need to reestablish a productive harmony with nature, one that satisfies both social and economic requirements for present and future generations.

When you go shopping next, take a moment out of your trip to pay attention to the products you purchase. Before you buy them again, assess their environmental impact. Read their labels and learn where that product came from before it hit those shelves. Choose only sustainable and eco-friendly options from here on out.

Remember what I said about its being difficult to identify true green products? Well, now that you know how to identify them, do they really exist in supermarkets? Are you going to find what you're looking for? If these products do exist, are they profitable to their manufacturers?

There are many different eco-friendly events all over the world that offer their guests the opportunity to experience true green products and services. For example, the VegFest Expo, produced by Experience Expositions, showcases hundreds of brands that adequately meet and uphold respectable levels of sustainability for everyday consumers. If you are interested, I strongly suggest you seek out a community near you that focuses on creating a sustainable future for our planet.

SUSTAINABILITY: THE ROLE OF NGOS AND INDIGENOUS COMMUNITIES

To achieve success in a sustainability campaign, we must first believe that this dream is 100 percent possible. We need to understand the impact our daily activities have on the environment. More important than just believing, we also need to understand that it does not have to be painful to live a green life. It is as simple as buying and using products and resources with sustainability fresh in our minds.

This part of our journey entails an important task that is being successfully implemented by various NGOs and other organizations around the world, such as 1% For the Planet, founded in 2002. Since its inception, it has become a global movement with over 1200 member companies from 48 countries. All these companies donate at least one percent of their sales to environmental groups, proudly claiming it as an "Earth Tax."

In 2001 and 2002, 1% For the Planet's global network surpassed $100 million in total donations towards environmental preservation. This organization has a firm focus on issues such as:

- Alternate modes of transportation

- Climate change

- Food

- Land

- Water

- Wildlife

Their mission ultimately is to build, support, and activate a coming together of businesses that are willing to financially back the dream for a healthy planet. Thus far, they have been successful in utilizing the support of businesses as mechanisms for positive environmental change.

This organization also helps in developing deep brand-aligned partnerships with nonprofit organizations and similar-minded companies. These members make donations right to their nonprofits. If a nonprofit is focused 50 percent or more on issues of sustainability, 1% For the Planet will be there to amplify its cause and gather the funding needed to support important causes.

More than 3,330 nonprofits

More than $100 million given back to blue

NATIVE AMERICANS: THE ORIGINAL CONSERVATIONISTS

Every seed is awakened and so has all animal life. It is through this mysterious power that we too have our being, and we therefore yield to our neighbors, even our animal neighbors, the same right as ourselves, to inhabit this land.

—Sitting Bull

The above words from Chief Sitting Bull are hopefully enough to illustrate the legendary environmental wisdom of the

Native Americans. With an increase of awareness among earth's populace about the need for sustainability, it is slowly becoming clearer that Native Americans were the original pure ecologists and conservationists of this nation. Their environmental ethics are something we must observe and practice to preserve this beautiful land for our future.

While Native Americans did hunt animals and cut down trees, they only did it for the bare necessities of food and shelter. They did not believe in the concept of private property, and all land was common land. Additionally, they had a love for nature and a belief that all plants and animals have a spirit that deserves to be revered. A native hunter would ask permission of the animal's spirit prior to hunting it, making it impossible for the hunter to kill for pleasure.

Chief Seattle's speech of 1854 still echoes this true love of nature:

Every part of this soil is sacred in the estimation of my people. Every hillside, every valley, every plain and grove, has been hallowed by some sad or happy event in days long vanished. Even the rocks, which seem to be dumb and dead as they swelter in the sun along the silent shore, thrill with memories of stirring events connected with the lives of my people, and the very dust upon which you now stand responds more lovingly to their footsteps than yours, because it is rich with the blood of our ancestors, and our bare feet are conscious of the sympathetic touch.

Their belief in pantheism provided Native Americans with a profound reverence for nature and the rest of the universe, guiding their actions by taking only what they needed from the environment, leaving the rest for future generations.

Currently, many Native Americans still hold onto these beliefs and do not hesitate to voice their love for nature and spread the ways to conserve it.

CHAPTER FOUR

DAILY HABITS THAT ARE KILLING THE ENVIRONMENT

"Sustainability is the key to our survival on this planet, and will also determine success on all levels."

—Shari Arison

While it might not seem like it, every little thing we do has an impact and leaves a footprint on the Earth around us. While we continuously destroy forestlands and decrease biodiversity, we are slowly threatening our very existence as we know it. To achieve a maximum level of human comfort, we have neglected to look at the gravity our actions have on this planet.

Most often, such actions are born out of ignorance. For instance, instead of using a reusable steel spoon, there are still those who choose plastic disposable cutlery. Though we know right from wrong, our focus is more on teaching new generations consumerism to the max. The quicker something reaches the trash, the sooner we purchase a replacement. Unfortunately, many manufacturers fail to consider the impact made by producing unrecyclable waste.

Therefore, the choice begins with us. Once we are armed with the knowledge of how our everyday actions impact the environment, we can strive to bring momentous change. Here are a few common events that take place in homes all around the globe that can contribute toward a sustainable planet.

LEAVING THE LIGHTS ON

If you are leaving a room, even if only for ten minutes, consider turning the lights off. This simple action will save generous amounts of energy that cannot be replaced. If you need a reminder, try putting up a sticky note to remind you to cut out the lights when you leave a room.

Today, we have several options regarding which light bulbs we use. Incandescent lights are the biggest wasters of energy with 90 percent of this energy released as heat. Therefore, if you turn them off when you don't need them, your home will be cooler, especially in the summer months. With a market that is being flooded with energy-efficient lights, you have plenty of room to choose better bulbs such as LEDs, halogens, or CFLs.

Though halogens and CFLs are much more energy efficient than your typical incandescent bulbs, light emitting diodes, or LEDs, are a more energy-efficient way to provide light.

Below are some examples of how this technology is so energy efficient:

- They shine in one distinct direction

- They produce a fraction of heat in comparison with incandescent bulbs or CFLs

LED lights produce their light when electrons pass through semi-conductors. LEDs don't just help with conserving energy, they also save you money for air-conditioning costs. To reap these benefits, you must invest in high-efficiency LED lighting. When you shop for LED lighting, you need to first look for an Energy Star rating. This rating is a joint program of the US EPA and Department of Energy and it labels only the LED lights that meet energy-efficient guidelines.

Currently, an LED light labeled "energy efficient" is required to consume 75 percent less energy than incandescent bulbs, lasting fifteen times longer. Your average operating cost of LED bulbs is about $1 a year, compared to $1.20 for Energy Star qualified CFL bulbs, $3.50 for halogen incandescent bulbs, and $4.80 for traditional incandescents.

Currently, an LED light labeled "energy efficient" is required to consume 75 percent less energy than incandescent bulbs, lasting fifteen times longer.

Current lighting technology presents a great deal of hope for future generations. A recent survey showed that one in every five people plan on purchasing LEDs for their home. Further, from 2012 to 2014, the consumption of LEDs has increased thirty fold. To make these products smarter, they can be fitted with sensors and cameras that provide expanded potential for applications such as facial recognition, and LED tech has also reached security applications. Within the estimated 400 million shipments of smart wireless lighting products in 2019, much of that inventory will be LED light bulbs.

After learning of the benefits of energy-efficient light bulbs, there are still those who complain about the slightly higher cost of LED lights. However, it is natural for a new product to be a bit more cost prohibitive compared to a product that has been on the shelves longer. In fact, the price of energy-efficient lighting has dropped, and is expected to soon match the price of other bulbs. On the bright side, the price of the LED bulb is fair when you consider how much energy it saves.

USING PLASTIC BAGS AND SPOONS

While it might be hard to consider, each time you see a

person with an armful of grocery bags, you are witnessing a major contribution to our overcrowded landfills. The same is true for those that utilize plastic and paper plates, cups, napkins, etc. It is wise to instead invest in roomy and convenient reusable cloth bags for your shopping trips as well as sustainable silverware.

Within the course of a year, we as Americans consume at least 100 billion cups of coffee. Over 16 billion of those coffees are purchased and served in disposable paper cups. To meet these demands, 6.5 million trees must be cut down. During manufacturing, 4 billion pounds of CO_2 are released into the atmosphere. In addition to other products, our love for coffee is also threatening the forests and our environment.

Now, I am sure you are asking yourself, "why can't these cups be recycled?" Well, the answer is simple. Most paper cups have a thin coating of polyethylene resin for strength and insulation. The addition of this coating completely rules out recycling. The same is true for Styrofoam cups that get left in landfills and never decompose. Unfortunately, it is estimated that 40 percent of solid waste in our landfills is paper and cardboard.

Choosing to use ceramic cups and plates is the eco-friendly approach. Although using ceramic plates, bowls, and cups has its own impact on the environment, it is considerably less than disposable utensils.

When you next visit your local coffee shop, be sure to ask for your coffee in a mug instead of a paper cup. While it might take more time for you to sit and enjoy your coffee, it could be your biggest contribution to the Earth that day.

The same goes for the plastic packaging on products bought from the grocery store or online. Try calling these companies and pleading with them to use less packaging on their products. We all need to do our part and support the organizations and brands that agree to make changes to their overall environmental impact.

SENDING BIODEGRADABLES TO LANDFILLS

It is not uncommon to see lots of biodegradable waste within landfills. There are many of us who will fill our trash cans with food peels, tea bags, and other reusable materials. Our laziness might be the reason behind this, or our ignorance of how to make better plans for our trash. For instance, certain waste materials can be used to create compost – and you do not need a garden to do it!

Start with a small container with a lid in the kitchen where you can begin placing peels and the like to start your compost.

LEAVING WATER RUNNING

From washing dishes to brushing our teeth, leaving the tap running is an unfortunate habit a lot of us have that wastes vast amounts of water. It might seem petty, but soaking dishes prior to washing them, and cutting off the water while brushing our teeth, will reduce your water use. Once again, Post-it notes can be helpful reminders.

Nearly one billion people in the developing world do not have access to clean and safe drinking water.

These simple water-saving tips are a wonderful way to work toward sustainability and a shared respect for those living without clean, safe drinking water. Nearly one billion people on Earth find it difficult to even wrangle up one glass of water, and suffer because of it.

Here are some more facts found by numerous studies performed by the United Nations and other nonprofits[7]:

• 85% of Earth's population lives on the drier half of the planet

• 783 million people do not have access to clean water, with 2.5 billion living without access to adequate sanitation

- 6 to 8 million people die annually from consequences of disasters and water-related disease

Water scarcity is only going to grow all over the world. A sizable percentage of clean water on Earth is utilized for farmland irrigation.

Here are a few statistics to get you thinking:

- To produce one pound of beef it takes approximately 2,500 gallons of water

- It takes close to 37 gallons of water to produce one cup of coffee

The sub-Saharan Africa region serves as the perfect example of how water scarcity can impact populations of people in developing countries such as India or Pakistan. Recently, receding groundwater levels in India have come into light as a real problem. Additionally, there is a presence of toxic pollutants like chlorine, fluoride, iron, nitrate, and arsenic that exceeds national safety limits. As a result, there are around 130 million people living in areas with unsafe levels of toxins. By 2030, it is estimated that the world's water supply will fall 50 percent below international demand.

As you can see, it is necessary for us to adopt sustainable attitudes, behaviors, and lifestyles. We can begin water conservation right in our own homes.

COMMUTING

Whether we commute to work each day or travel abroad on business trips, the way in which we choose to travel plays a significant role in environmental pollution. Interestingly enough, a 60-mile road trip in a car burns almost the same amount of fuel per passenger as a five-hour cross country flight. However, flying also requires environmental consideration for a variety of reasons. For instance:

- Planes emit more harmful gases than just carbon dioxide

- When gases are released at these heights, the harmful impact is much greater than gases released at ground level – also known as the "radiative forcing" effect

Just a few cross-country flights are equal to the average American's commute for the entire year.

This is one of the many reasons why the European Union, for example, adopted aviation into its emissions control plan circa 2008. As a result, several airline companies are working on decreasing their carbon footprint, adopting technological advancements into the construction of planes. A trade group for United States carriers by the name of Airlines for America has proposed setting emissions targets for flights by 2020. While these habits might not be completely avoidable all the time, we can at least take steps toward reducing activities that are harmful to the environment. Simple things like not using our cars so much, carpooling, or walking/cycling are a good start. Make sure you drive within the speed limit as much as possible, as fuel economy decreases rapidly at high speeds. Additionally, fully inflated tires can save on fuel.

THE USE OF HEAVY CHEMICAL PESTICIDES AND HERBICIDES

While pesticides and herbicides might be an immense help to our lawns and gardens, these toxic substances have high chances of getting mixed with water sources. Often this results in the creation of hypoxic "dead zones" within oceans and large lakes, making it impossible for even fish to survive.

By reducing the chemical dependency of your plants, you can keep them thriving with fertilizers and compost. If you garden for food, you will soon be enjoying toxin-free fruits and veggies.

Companies like Monsanto are really to blame here. They single-handedly spearheaded the campaign for genetically engineered crops. They trademarked RoundUp, which is mainly used on genetically engineered crops, and is responsible for 90 percent of the genetically engineered traits that have led the way to grave concern among health and environmental experts.

In the United States, almost 90 percent of crop seeds produced are engineered to withstand RoundUp.

When this concept was first introduced in the 90s, it promised such features as:

- Increased production

- Resistance toward climate change

- Elevated levels of nutrition

- Minimal use of herbicides/pesticides

Currently, experts are pointing out these crops' ability to withstand a weed killer like RoundUp. It is estimated that in the US, almost 90 percent of crop seeds are engineered to withstand RoundUp. Since the introduction of these GM seeds and crops, there has been a notable rise in the use of glyphosate. For example: the use of glyphosate (RoundUp) on only two crops like corn and soy has increased about 17 times from 1996 to 2012. So, it grew from roughly 12.5 million pounds to 210 million pounds.

So how is this situation affecting sustainability? According to recent research by the World Health Organization International Agency for Research on Cancer (IARC), glyphosate is "probably carcinogenic to humans." Soon after this research was released, Columbia stopped the use of glyphosate as a part of its cancer eradication program. Countries like Sri Lanka and Bermuda have completely banned the import of glyphosate products.

Apart from the possible harm to humans, consistent use of RoundUp has led to the emergence of "super weeds" which cannot be eradicated by glyphosate.

EATING FARMED MEAT

To feed cattle on farms, multiple acres of soy and grain are cut down. Therefore, by consuming farmed meat, you are supporting one of the most environmentally detrimental industries. While it's not easy to adopt a vegan/vegetarian lifestyle, you can contribute to this cause by simply consuming less. If you visit your local grocery store, there are plant-based meat alternatives. Research proves that greenhouse gas emissions are reduced by going meatless one day a week, and this reduction is equal to driving a 20-mpg vehicle for just 16.5 miles. Most of these meat substitutes are manufactured from soy protein, pea protein isolates, yeast, and other ingredients.

There are several other activities that have an adverse impact on the environment. Here are some examples of some behaviors that can help curb our negative impact on Earth:

- Reduce, reuse, recycle, and compost

- Conserve energy

- Cut emissions and reduce use of toxic chemicals

- Conserve water

- Preserve wilderness, educate, and advocate

It is imperative that we stay informed and keep an eye on political and commercial developments that can have an impact on our environment. These practices will help us to make informed decisions and raise our voices for the planet.

CHAPTER FIVE

STRIVING TO MAKE SUSTAINABLE PRODUCTS

"Never doubt that a small group of thoughtful, committed citizens can change the world; indeed, it's the only thing that ever has."

—Margaret Mead

In our current world, it is important for us to come together despite race, culture, religion, or personal beliefs in order to create a sustainable Earth.

One of the first steps toward creating a green world is creating sustainable, eco-friendly products. Second, consumers should feel the need to buy them; having them on shelves is not enough.

We as consumers must be educated on the choices we make, as well as which ones can contribute to the survival of our planet. We need more and more companies to be attracted to this path, witnessing more green products becoming a success. Scientists, engineers, designers, and business strategists must work together if they wish to work toward making sustainable products for a sustainable world. The three vital steps toward sustainability include:

- Creating eco-friendly products

- Creating an educated base of consumers

- Marketing products

It is vital for us to understand these three parts if we ever want to concrete a plan for our planet.

DESIGNING FOR SUSTAINABILITY (D4S):

Companies across the globe must innovate their products and processes alike to keep up with the following:

- Competitive pressure

- Increasing productivity within their region

- Expanding their market share

- Attracting foreign investors

Unfortunately, it is easy for companies in developing countries to be left out of this cycle for a variety of economic and structural reasons.

Product innovation is becoming a key move available to firms, supply chains, and industrial sectors within these developing countries so they can compete in the global market. Local and international markets are additionally gaining ground through advancements in information, communication, and infrastructure.

Interest in product innovation has grown rapidly within the past few decades. Industrialization, open markets, higher quality requirements from customers, and an increase in competitiveness between local and global companies have formed a very real demand for a concrete process for product innovation. These industries cannot survive without product innovation being integrated into company management.

Several medium to large companies have at least one product innovation specialist on their management teams. For example, consider Apple which has its own sustainability initiative team. In developing countries, the importance of product innovation is growing. For instance, in India their market has officially opened to international competition, so product innovation has become an imperative discipline.

With concerns about environmental problems growing globally, sustainability approaches are quickly being adapted everywhere. Governments, industries, and civil societies have in turn adopted terms for sustainable consumption and production.

D4S is based upon the combination of product innovation and sustainability

Design for sustainability, or D4S, is one of the more useful tools for enterprises and governments to deal with these concerns, including the concept of eco-design. In other words, companies are incorporating environmental and social factors into product development, throughout the supply chain, and with respect to their socio-economic surroundings.

Companies big and small have previously attempted to address the lack of sustainability through supply chain management, corporate reporting, and the adoption of international standards. Now, in addition, companies are increasing efficiency of current production and designing around consumer needs. The concept of D4S or eco-design is globally recognized to improve product quality and market opportunities while embracing sustainability. Design for sustainability goes further than the creation of green products. This concept efficiently meets consumer needs along with social, economic, and environmental needs.

CHAPTER SIX

MAINSTREAMING THE GREENER PRODUCTS

"Out of all those millions and millions of planets floating around there in space, this is our planet, this is our little one, so we just got to be aware of it and take care of it."

—Paul McCartney

One of the toughest issues companies are dealing with is trying to sell eco-friendly products while we as consumers neglect to act on our "green intentions." Recent studies show that 82 percent of Americans have eco-friendly intentions, however, just 16 percent fulfill these intentions.

The disconnect between our desire for sustainability and the follow through is a growing concern among environmentalists and top corporations which have invested in the research, manufacturing, and sale of sustainable goods.

These realizations have forced non-government and government organizations to focus on the right way to spread the message of sustainability. Through awareness, we can change the buying nature of consumers everywhere.

GREEN PRODUCTS: NOT FOR US

One of the key reasons behind this issue is the thought process among consumers that going green or working toward sustainability is not a matter for the everyday American. We often mistake this as something only important to the government or nature enthusiasts. However, this is something that depends on each one of us.

GREEN PRODUCTS: TOO COSTLY

The price tag that comes along with most green products in comparison to your everyday products is another reason why we seem to avoid them.

The global economic state of affairs also has an impact on our way of thinking in relation to green products. Most people would rather pay their bills on time than worry about spending money on expensive green products.

GREEN WORLD: GENDER INEQUALITY

As irrational as it sounds, there are people who view green as the new pink, so to speak. Recent studies prove 82 percent of respondents think that going green is emasculating. This falsely perceived feminism is causing men to think twice about behaviors like using reusable water bottles or reusable grocery bags.

LACK OF BELIEF IN GREEN PRODUCTS

Considering the short amount of time that green products have been on the market, there is a lack of credibility among consumers, which is to be expected. People have natural worries like whether the use of green products will leave their children susceptible to more viruses, or if kids use their bikes instead of being driven, will they be more prone to getting hit by cars? Ultimately, many of us feel like practicing sustainability compromises our comforts. Being that the governments, NGOs, and corporations have neglected to get the message of sustainability out to consumers, this disconnect has also worsened.

TICKLE THE EMOTIONAL PART OF THE BRAIN

Many of us do not buy products to save the environment. Multiple studies prove that decision-making happens within the emotional part of our brains. Basically, that means facts alone are not enough to help us make the right choice regarding buying green. To spread the message of sustainability, we must appeal to the feelings, senses, perceptions, and beliefs of consumers.

Successfully marketing a green product relies heavily on the product's advantages and benefits, and less on the "save the Earth" aspect. Additionally, many of us are not heavily concerned with the plight of polar bears. Instead, bringing in local examples is the way to go.

Green products should additionally not give off the feeling that they are simply for fundraising purposes. Instead, they need to focus on health, comfort, convenience, lifestyle, and beauty.

THE KEYS: MANUFACTURING PRACTICES, INGREDIENTS, AND PACKAGING

More attention must be paid to the way products are packaged. Many of us skip over that and read for certifications and ingredients used during manufacturing. Other things we should look for include:

- Recycling

- No chemical waste

- Renewable energy

- Minimal packaging

- Sustainable life cycles

For food, these aspects are a bit different:

- Vegan or plant-based

- Contains no chemicals/preservatives

- Not genetically modified

- No additives or pesticides

- Contains only natural ingredients

It is easy for a leading brand to gain attention with green alternatives due to its preexisting reputation as a brand. It's important to people to believe in a company. Without this confidence in a product or manufacturer, all green certifications fall by the wayside.

SENDING THE RIGHT MESSAGE

Many of us do not believe that the companies claiming product sustainability are actually working toward sustainable development. This is due in large part to the fact that companies in the past tended to underestimate the consumer. Contradictions in statements or advertising can quickly erase the company's image as a promoter of a green ideology.

BRIBE SHAMELESSLY AND PUNISH WISELY

While buying green products should be rewarded, the real guilt of destroying our home should be motivation enough. Companies can encourage this behavior by offering discounts or freebies for current or future purchases.

MANAGING THE PRICE

One of the first steps toward lowering the high price of eco-friendly products is to eliminate a sustainability tax. This tax provides the consumer with the feeling that the company is attempting to restrict sustainable choices. We must decrease these prices if green products are to make it into the mainstream.

There is a good chance that once prices are lowered, we will see an increase in interest in green products among consumers. This will in turn increase demand, lower prices, and make them affordable for the everyday American.

When marketing to the consumer, green products must present the fact that they are simple and beneficial for consumers. We also must realize that at basically the same price, we are able to make an eco-friendly choice that can provide both health and happiness for our beautiful planet and future generations alike.

CHAPTER SEVEN

WHY FOCUS ON GREENER PRODUCTS?

"It was not until we saw the picture of the earth from the moon that we realized how small and how helpless this planet is – something that we must hold in our arms and care for."

—Margaret Mead

The necessity behind the focus on greener products is greater than ever before. As I mentioned earlier, however, it is somewhat difficult for us to make the connection between the downfall of the environment and our daily actions. And, even though we hear words like 'eco-friendly' and 'sustainability' every day, something prevents us from making such practices an integral part of our lives. The world we know has yet to understand the essence of a sustainable life.

These facts are perhaps the reason we spot so many consumers filling their carts with sustainable products, loading them into plastic bags, and driving home in their SUVs. So where does the real problem lie? Does it start with our lack of awareness, or the lack of commitment we feel towards such a substantial change?

Experts have shown that many of us buy green products because we believe they will help our families or save us money. Therefore, the connection between the consumer and green products is a personal one. Rather than worrying about how a product is impacting the environment, we are, of course, more concerned with how it benefits our family.

In some respects, the current thought process among consumers is both forward-thinking and positive. Although we still need to learn a bit about our responsibility toward the environment, our current situation provides us the opportunity to make people realize the true value in green products.

Our efforts toward rebuilding the planet could potentially build a sustainable future for our children and their children. We must educate ourselves and those around us on a sustainable way of life that takes care of our planet, and in the long run, takes care of future generations as well. The more we practice eco-friendly behaviors, the more they will become our reality.

BUYING GREEN PRODUCTS

Globalization in recent years has helped to bring the world together, making it seem smaller as we are all interconnected. Therefore, we have so many goods that are made in China, Argentina, etc. As a result, our actions on either side of the globe have an impact on one another. For instance, a toy made in China can have an impact on the health of our own nation's toddlers. Additionally, you might be surprised to learn that greenhouse gas emissions can affect the diminishing rain forests in Brazil. Because we share an ecosystem, so too do we share the responsibility of caring for it properly. Only a collective effort can get the job done.

I conceive that the land belongs to a vast family of which many are dead, few are living, and countless numbers are still unborn.

ORGANIC FOOD: A TERRIFIC WAY TO STAY GREEN AND HEALTHY

The best practice to stay healthy is to purchase mostly seasonal, local, and organic foods. Researchers explain that a product like organic almond milk is more nutritious than conventional milk. For example, it contains 68 percent more omega-3 fatty acids. A healthy, organic diet will do your body wonders.

Apart from adopting a healthy diet that is highly beneficial to your mental and physical health, this practice will also boost the economy, promote local agriculture, and advocate for responsible land use. Additionally, it helps to reduce the carbon footprint of the harvest and processing of food.

Even if you live in the city and do not have much room, you can create a terrace or kitchen garden with a little work and innovation. Growing your own food is not only relaxing, but also delicious.

KEEPING YOUR SKIN GLOWING BY GOING GREEN

By the year 2018, it is projected that the global revenue of the skincare industry will reach around $102 billion. Our skin consumes up to 60 percent of the products we use, and often they contain toxic elements. Even all-natural, organic skincare products cannot always be trusted. By law, companies with organic labels are supposed to utilize only organic ingredients. Unfortunately, a lot of companies get around this by stating that their product contains only "organic substances," even when it is only 70 percent organic. This means that 30 percent could contain toxic elements.

There are major loopholes in United States federal law that allow the skincare industry to use toxic chemicals without even testing them first. It is alarming, but the U.S. government has only documented and studied 11 percent of 10,500 ingredients used in personal care products.

Here are some of the more common toxins used in cosmetics[8]:

• Coal tar – This is a known carcinogen that is banned in the EU. However, we still use it in North America. It is most often used in dry skin treatments, anti-lice, and anti-dandruff shampoos.

•   Formaldehyde – This irritant is found in nail products, hair dye, eyelash adhesives, and shampoos. This one is also banned in the EU.

•   DEA/TEA/MEA – These are suspected carcinogens that are used in shampoo, body wash, and soap.

•   Lead – This infamous carcinogen is found in lipsticks and hair dye, but is not listed as an ingredient.

•   Hydroquinone – This is a chemical that is used to lighten skin. It is rated most toxic on EWG's Skin Deep database and is linked to cancer and reproductive toxicity.

•   Mercury – A known allergen that impairs brain development and is linked to cancer, endocrine, and reproductive problems.

•   Parabens – This preservative is found in many hygienic products and is linked to cancer and reproductive problems.

•   Talc – Found in baby powder, eye shadow, blush, etc., this element is linked to ovarian cancer and respiratory problems.

Here are alternative ways to take care of yourself the green way:

•   Homemade beauty treatments are the way to go.

•   Read labels before you buy products, and check for unregulated chemicals.

•   Select your hair care products carefully as many of them contain carcinogens.

•   Look for petroleum-free products. Cutting down on your use of fossil fuels is critical in going green. You would be surprised to learn how many cosmetics and personal care products containing petroleum, mineral oils, etc.

AVOIDING ENERGY CONSUMING PRODUCTS

By choosing eco-friendly clothing, you can save the world's most chemically-dependent crops and can also choose a better product that is easier on the soil and groundwater.

Choosing to walk, ride a bike, or take public transportation, helps in reducing your carbon footprint by reducing or eliminating the emission of carbon dioxide and other particulate emissions created by driving a gas- or diesel-powered car.

Today, it is possible to purchase eco-friendly alternatives from an ever-expanding variety of products across all industries: energy efficient cars, organic foods, eco-friendly fashions, solar energy, green beauty products, eco-friendly toys and diapers, green construction and building materials, etc. A rise in demand for green products will force other companies to also move towards sustainable practices, revising their production standards accordingly.

The change is already visible; it is our responsibility to make the movement into a revolution that will ensure future generations' comfortable existence on this planet.

CHAPTER EIGHT

DRIVERS & BARRIERS FOR SUSTAINABILITY

"If we each take responsibility in shifting our own behavior, we can trigger the type of change that is necessary to achieve sustainability for our race or this planet. We change our planet, our environment, our humanity every day, every year, every decade, and every millennium."

—Yehuda Berg

Sustainability is fast becoming a concept that many of us are trying to understand. However, it is hard to determine how much of this enthusiasm gets translated into action. In the following chapter, we will discuss the key drivers and barriers faced by a world attempting sustainability.

DRIVERS OF SUSTAINABILITY

Driving forces are a range of factors that induce retailers to undertake certain activities. They help retailers to initiate, maintain, and expand sustainable businesses. These factors include:

- Financial incentives

- Strategic opportunities to enter the green market

- Regulatory incentives

- Organizational values and top management commitments

We will discuss these points in detail in the next few chapters.

BARRIERS OF SUSTAINABILITY

The costs of actions to reduce environmental impacts can be a barrier for retailers (BIO Intelligence Service, 2009).

Another factor argued as a reason for the lack of sustainable activities implemented at the business level is the lack of training and information among the lower levels of the organization.

Secondly, there is often a lack of a robust business plan that arises from conflicting business priorities between procurement, marketing, and environmental teams within the company itself.

Another barrier is the lack of an independent measure for evaluating sustainability efforts in the retail sector: without such an independent assessment, retailers can make a variety of claims which are difficult for consumers to verify, value, or even compare.

However, retailers generally do not favor such regulations due to the cost implications, particularly when regulations differ between countries. It is not necessary that substances banned in Europe face the same situation in the US or in any of the other emerging markets across the globe.

However, even after the arrival of all these barriers, the world is witnessing a surge in the number of green products both at the market and product-design levels. Credit for this must be given to the thousands of volunteers and NGOs working tirelessly toward educating the population on the impact of green products and sustainability on our beautiful planet.

CHAPTER NINE

MARKET DRIVERS FOR GREENER PRODUCTS

"Anything else you're interested in is not going to happen if you can't breathe the air and drink the water. Don't sit this one out. Do something."

—Carl Sagan

Concern for our environment is not a new phenomenon. Waves of environmental concern have arisen over the years, with different concerns at various times. This time, however, it's different. It is different in the readiness of people to embrace the concept of sustainability, visible in many ways, including the wide variety of green products available today.

The rise in environmental concerns among socially conscious consumers has been a focal point of research in recent years. The focus has been on:

- The level of understanding an average consumer has about green products, and

- How people respond, as consumers, to sustainability challenges.

These factors must be understood as, together, they form the key for deciding what market strategies to use for a product. Knowledge of consumer behaviors can help companies to position themselves.

With every passing day, there is an increase in the number of players, making it even more important to understand the key market drivers for green or eco-friendly consumer products.

PRODUCT PRESENTATION MATTERS

A few years ago, it was hard to find enough products to satisfy a consumer in search of green products. For instance, my search for a green household cleaner led me to products from three different companies: Mrs. Meyer's, Method, and Seventh Generation. These products are eco-friendly, so how could I choose between the three? There is a clear link between the choice to buy and a presentable package. Having packaging made from recyclable materials is a great start.

GREEN CONSUMERISM

Let there be no doubt that an aware population is a better consumer of green products than a population which does not have much knowledge about such products or the concept of sustainability.

Most Americans say that it is important that the products they purchase be environmentally friendly, such as automobiles (66% say it is important or essential to them), clothes detergent (62%), and computer printer paper (51%). When asked if price or eco-friendly stats matter most to them, consumers in this study chose the green option.

PUBLIC VIEWS ON A SELECTION OF GREEN PRODUCTS[9]

% OF RESPONDENTS AGREEING WITH THE STATEMENT
It is essential/important that products purchased be eco-friendly.

- Automobile   66%

- Clothes detergent   62%

- Computer printer paper   51%

- Wood furniture   40%

Eco-friendliness is more important than quality or price when purchasing.

- Automobile   17%

- Clothes detergent   23%

- Computer paper   26%

- Wood furniture   11%

I would definitely or probably pay 15% more for eco-friendly products.

- Automobile   50%

- Clothes detergent   51%

- Computer printer paper   40%

- Wood furniture   39%

While the above may seem like a paradox, there lies within a market driver. As per a variety of studies based around green products and consumer behavior, consumers have been divided into five categories:

- LOHAS (Lifestyles of Health and Sustainability): Active stewards of the environment; dedicated to personal and planetary health; lifestyle-oriented; heaviest purchasers of green/socially responsible products.

- Naturalites: Secondary targets for many mainstream LOHAS products; personal health motivated; more likely to use LOHAS consumables than durables; income restricts some behavior, creating attitudinal versus behavioral disconnects.

• Drifters: Good intentions; some barriers with follow through; trendy and price sensitive.

• Conventionals: Practical; Yankee ingenuity (self-reliance); conservation-oriented.

• Unconcerned: Unconcerned about the environment or society.

Companies should design green products and marketing strategies keeping the first three segments of consumers in mind. Fortunately, over the years, there has been a steady increase in the percentage of LOHAS consumers, thanks to widespread sustainability awareness programs, workshops, and fairs.

Though it may take a while before eco-friendly products start to capture major market shares, this category of products is witnessing a steady increase of consumers. The global market for low carbon environmental goods and services is estimated at $4.7 trillion.

The United States Organic Food Market Forecast & Opportunities 2018 states that the country's organic food market is estimated to grow 14 percent from 2013-18. It also points to the fact that about 81 percent of American families have organic food at least sometimes.

The report further sheds light on fast-growing domestic organic food production (240 percent between 2002-2012 when compared to 30 percent for non-organic food). The steadily rising demand for organic food is a good sign for believers in sustainability.

PUBLIC VIEWS ON A SELECTION OF GREEN PRODUCTS

The global organic foods and beverages market size reached USD 91 billion in 2015. The increasing awareness about health benefits associated with consumption of organic products is expected to drive the demand over the forecast period

GREEN POLICIES

Policies and frameworks encouraging companies and institutions to make sustainable, eco-friendly choices, have been part of our system for years. For instance, the US Resource Conservation and Recovery Act of 1976 requires federal agencies to establish affirmative procurement programs for EPA-designated recycled content products.

However, it has only been in recent years that both the government and companies have started to give importance to such policies. From being just clauses on paper, they have risen to greater market significance.

Faced with large-scale problems such as climate change, rising energy prices, and chemical exposure and liability, many companies, large institutions, and even consumers, are looking to reduce risk and/or contribute positively within their own particular spheres of influence.

Further, green credentials are fast becoming important market-access determinants. An eco-market Summary Report of 2009[10] surveyed 587 professional purchasers in the United States and Canada whose organizations spend more than $68 billion each year, and they had the following insights into the changing approach towards sustainability:

• 72% of purchasers said their organization has implemented either a formal (29%) or informal (43%) green purchasing policy, up from 63% in 2008 (26% formal and 37% informal).

• Of the 28% of purchasers who work for organizations without a green purchasing policy, 54% indicated their organization had plans to implement one, up from 44% in 2008.

There may be many product characteristics that influence consumer choice: special features, performance, design, brand image, price, availability, etc. However, time and again, some of the key facts that the makers of the product highlight are outright dismissed by consumers.

The same is the case with green products.

The journey of introducing and marketing a green product has been a bit confusing, from the manufacturers' point of view. While it has been hard to point at reasons leading to a product's success or failure, manufacturers have nevertheless been patient enough to bring one eco-friendly product after the other to market. At least they have started to realize that it is here that the future lies.

CHAPTER TEN

REGULATORY DRIVERS FOR GREENER PRODUCTS

"Innovations that are guided by smallholder farmers, adapted to local circumstances, and sustainable for the economy as well as environment, will be necessary to ensure food security in the future."

—Bill Gates

The passing of many green regulations has led the companies to develop management systems that ensure that the product being brought to the market complies with the number of laws pertaining to design, reporting, labeling, and fee requirements across the globe.

ISO STANDARDS[11]

ISO 14021 standard, which was introduced in 1999 by the International Organization for Standardization (ISO), is about self-declared environmental claims. It focuses on both preventing deception and encouraging products that cause less stress on the environment.

The recently published ISO environmental packaging standards are the following:

• ISO 18601:2013 Packaging and the environment — General requirements for the use of ISO standards in the field of packaging and the environment.

• ISO 18602:2013 Packaging and the environment — Optimization of the packaging system.

• ISO 18603:2012 Packaging and the environment — Reuse.

• ISO 18604:2013 Packaging and the environment — Material recycling.

• ISO 18605:2013 Packaging and the environment — Energy recovery.

• ISO 18606:2013 Packaging and the environment — Organic recycling.

EU FRAMEWORK[12]

For instance, the EU Packaging and Packaging Waste Directive (94/62/EC) contains "essential requirements" to prevent production of packaging waste and to increase recycling of packaging materials.

• EN 13427:2004, Packaging requirements for the use of European Standards in the field of packaging and packaging waste.

• EN 13428:2004, Packaging requirements specific to manufacturing and composition prevention by source reduction.

• EN 13430:2004, Packaging requirements for packaging recoverable by material recycling.

• EN 13431:2004, Packaging requirements for packaging recoverable in the form of energy recovery, including specification of minimum inferior calorific value.

• EN 13432:2000, Packaging requirements for packaging recoverable through composting and biodegradation test scheme and evaluation criteria for the final acceptance of packaging.

ICC's framework defines a green or environmental claim as any type of claim where "explicit or implicit reference is made to the environmental or ecological aspects relating to the production, packaging, distribution, use/consumption, or disposal of products." The extent of the obligations placed on industry sectors will vary depending on the quantity of each chemical substance manufactured in, exported to, or incorporated into finished products exported to Europe by each affected company, and on the hazard properties of the chemical substance.

Extended Producer Responsibility (EPR), as a principle of product policy, was first introduced into law in the early 1990s to address the lifecycle issues of products, especially what happens to them at the end of their life and using a target- oriented approach, instead of traditional command-and-control type regulation.

In other words, EPR or "Producer Takeback" is a product and waste management system in which manufacturers – not the consumer or government – take responsibility for the environmentally safe management of a product when it is no longer useful or is discarded.

Since the introduction of EPR 20 years ago in Europe, a vast majority of EU Member States have introduced EPR for packaging, although the form of implementation varies from one country to the next, ranging from mandatory regulations to voluntary agreements between government and industry to voluntary industry initiatives.

Twenty-five states have already passed laws requiring producer responsibility, and many others are currently working towards passing producer responsibility laws.

CHAPTER ELEVEN

GREENER PRODUCT DESIGN PROGRAMS

"The future is green energy, sustainability, renewable energy."

—Arnold Schwarzenegger

Being energy efficient means both designing for efficiency and choosing the right technologies and energy sources. There are tons of companies putting out products they claim are green or otherwise eco-friendly. The big question here is: how can we, the consumers, be sure that a product is true to its promise of sustainable efforts?

The answer is simple: it comes in the form of programs and certifications that assess life cycles of products, from manufacturing to the trash. This cycle is known as the "cradle to the grave" analysis. See the diagram on the next page for a closer look.

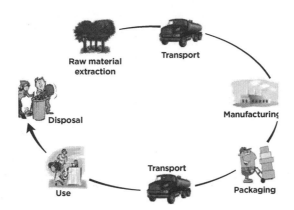

Common boundaries for life cycle assessment

LIST OF GREEN PROGRAMS

The following are the most commonly known green product design programs.

• Established by the EPA in 1992, ENERGY STAR is a voluntary program that helps businesses and individuals save money and protect our climate through superior energy efficiency.

• As of 2005, section 131 of the Act Amends Section 324 (42 USC 6294) of the Energy Policy and Conservation Act established a voluntary program at the Department of Energy and the Environmental Protection Agency to identify at the Department of Energy and the Environmental Protection Agency a voluntary program to identify and promote energy efficient products and buildings in order to reduce energy consumption, improve energy security, and reduce pollution through voluntary labeling of or other forms of communication about products and buildings that meet the highest energy efficiency standards.

• The ENERGY STAR program has helped in boosting the adoption of energy efficient products, practices, and services through valuable partnerships, objective measurement tools, and consumer education.

To maintain consumer trust and improve the oversight of ENERGY STAR-certified products, homes, and commercial facilities, the EPA has implemented third party certification requirements and testing.

In order to earn the label, ENERGY STAR products must be third-party certified based on testing in EPA-recognized laboratories. Additionally, to verify a home's energy efficiency, testing by a third-party organization is needed for receiving the ENERGY STAR. There are two paths to certify a home:

• The Prescriptive Path, based on a predefined package of improvements

• The Performance Path, based on a customized package of upgrades

Both the Performance and Prescriptive Paths require completion of four inspection checklists:

- Thermal Enclosure System Rater Checklist

- HVAC System Quality Installation Rater Checklist

- HVAC System Quality Installation Contractor Checklist

- Water Management System Builder Checklist

For an industrial plant to be eligible for ENERGY STAR, a professional engineer must certify that the information used to calculate the plant's 75 or higher energy performance score is correct.

The ENERGY STAR has a broad range of 16,000 partners across every sector, which include manufacturers, trade associations, retailers and efficiency program providers, home builders, and small businesses. Families and companies across America are improving the energy efficiency of their homes and businesses with help from ENERGY STAR in ways that cost less and help the environment.

This success is possible because ENERGY STAR continues to deliver on its promise to America of cost-effective, relevant, and high quality energy efficiency solutions.

The Green Electronics Council maintains the Electronic Products Environmental Assessment Tool (EPEAT) which is a comprehensive global environmental rating system that helps purchasers identify greener computers and other electronics. It helps purchasers evaluate, compare, and select electronic products based on their environmental attributes.

EPEAT[13]:

The Green Electronics Council maintains the Electronic Products Environmental Assessment Tool (EPEAT) which is a global environmental rating system that helps purchasers identify green electronics. With EPEAT we can assess, compare, and choose electronics based on their environmental statistics.

EPEAT product registration is country-specific because product identification and environmental performance can vary by location. Registration by country enables potential buyers around the world to evaluate, compare, and select the exact product models available to them based on the environmental characteristics that products attain in their country of purchase.

REGISTRATION OF PRODUCTS

EPEAT-registered products meet strict environmental criteria that address the full product life cycle, from energy conservation and toxic materials to product longevity and end-of-life management.

The Design for the Environment (DfE) Program began in the early 1990s as an innovative, non-regulatory initiative to help companies consider human health, environmental, and economic effects of chemicals and technologies, as well as product performance, when designing and manufacturing commercial products and processes.

Safer Choice (formerly known as DfE's Standard for Safer Products) works with manufacturers and helps consumers, businesses, and purchasers to find products that perform well and are safer for human health and the environment.

It currently has more than 2,000 recognized products that meet its stringent criteria for human and environmental health and can use the Safer Choice label.

In the mid-2000s—to add incentive to the chemical selection process—DfE developed a certification program based on its Standard for Safer Products and safer chemical criteria.

It would allow companies to differentiate their products in the marketplace and make it easier for consumers and business purchasers to identify safer products for people, families, and the environment.

In February 2015, the Safer Choice label replaced the DfE product label.

If you see this label on a product, especially cleaners and detergents, understand that every ingredient in the product has been reviewed by EPA scientists.

In addition to safer ingredients, Safer Choice products also include requirements for compliance with the most recent version of the Safer Choice Standard (reference Safer Choice Implementation and Compliance Schedules). They include:

• WaterSense-labeled products help you to reduce your water use while enjoying exceptional performance

• Provide consumers with easy ways to save water, as both a label for products and an information resource to help people use water more efficiently

• The product manufacturer enters into a WaterSense partnership agreement with EPA

• Upgrading to more efficient WaterSense-labeled products can help save billions of gallons of water in the country every year

Launched in 2004, SmartWay is an EPA program for the freight transportation sector that improves supply chain efficiency by reducing transportation-related emissions that affect climate change.

The program has also developed a comprehensive training curriculum to help other countries implement their own green freight programs.

Plug-In to eCycling is a partnership program between EPA and leading consumer electronics manufacturers, retailers, and mobile service providers that fostered and promoted opportunities for individuals to donate or recycle their electronics.

This program encouraged the responsible management of used electronics by challenging manufacturers and retailers to voluntarily commit to sending 100 percent of used electronics collected for reuse and recycling to third-party certified recyclers, and increased the total amount of used electronics collected.

EPA's Responsible Appliance Disposal (RAD) Program is a voluntary partnership program that helps protect the ozone layer and reduce emissions of greenhouse gases.

As part of the program, EPA serves as a technical clearinghouse on responsible appliance disposal program development and implementation; calculates annual and cumulative program benefits in terms of ODS and GHG emission savings and equivalents and, as available, potential cost savings; and provides partner recognition for achievement, such as through press releases, brochures, articles, and awards.

Established in 1994, the Pesticide Environmental Stewardship Program (PESP) is an EPA partnership program that works with the nation's pesticide-user community to promote Integrated Pest Management (IPM) practices.

The program supports the increased adoption of Integrated Pest Management (IPM) which, when done correctly, can reduce the need for pesticides.

EPA's Pesticide Program is a key federal partner in implementing the National Integrated Pest Management (IPM) Roadmap, which was developed collaboratively by several federal agencies, including the EPA; Department of Agriculture (USDA); Department of Interior (DOI); Department of Defense (DOD); US Agency for International Development (USAID); and the Department of Housing and Urban Development (HUD).

The program assists the pesticide-user community in

transitioning to Integrated Pest Management (IPM) practices in response to EPA Office of Pesticide Programs (OPP) regulations and priorities.

Through grants and partnerships, EPA's Pesticide Program has funded projects that assist pesticide users to adapt to OPP's regulatory decisions with alternatives that are both cost-effective and perform as well as or better than most products and practices.

CHAPTER TWELVE

CORPORATE SUSTAINABILITY TRENDS TO WATCH

"The concept of corporate social responsibility (CSR) has long been used as an effective lens through which to examine the actions business can take toward ensuring mutual long-term well-being and sustainability."

—Klaus Schwab

If the business community across the globe has any plans to thrive in the future, it is time that they start thinking about the steps to be taken to grow in harmony with the natural environment to provide a sustainable future for upcoming generations before it is too late.

ECO-FRIENDLY CELEBRITIES[14]

More and more celebrities are using their life in the limelight as a tool to spread the message on meaningful causes like environmental sustainability. Let us look at a few of such inspiring celebrities:

- Leonardo DiCaprio: Climate change

This prolific actor spends a lot of time on his Twitter handle discussing climate change and global warming, as well as renewable energy. His speech at the UN Climate Summit and his recent two million dollar donation to causes such as Oceans 5, raised widespread awareness of issues that need tackling today.

- Matt Damon: Sustainability of water

A co-founder of Water.org along with Gary White, Damon has been working to pioneer new solutions, financing models, transparency, and partnerships within the water sector.

A different approach from the standard charity model, Water. org, has been transforming lives for more than twenty years. Recently, to raise awareness of the global water crisis, and to help provide solutions, Belgian beer maker Stella Artois launched its first global social impact campaign, "Buy a Lady a Drink," with the support of Water.org.

- Gisele Bündchen: Environment conservation

Apart from being one of the most beautiful faces in the world, she is also a strong advocate for the conservation of drinkable water. Named the 2011 Greenest International Celebrity of the Year, Bündchen devotes an extraordinary amount of her time and money to environmental causes.

This ad is notable for veering from the typical approach of cause campaigns by using humor instead of emotional appeals to guilt consumers or donors to action.

HUMOR: THE BEST TOOL TO SAVE THE WORLD[15]

In the world of sustainability and cause-related marketing, we've come to expect a certain look and feel associated with green or organic. But, this fresh and humor-induced change has been accepted by people across the age groups.

There is an evolution occurring in the field of sustainability and cause marketing, a latent realization that cause, like traditional marketing, needs to be provocative, disruptive, and risk-taking in order to stand out.

With more and more leading brands showing their interest in being part of such campaigns, consumers are growing closer to the idea of sustainability. For instance, McDonald's in Australia is now proactively addressing customer questions. This new concept invites big brands to take part in the peer-to-peer economy in several ways.

SHIFTING PRODUCT PORTFOLIOS WITH SUSTAINABILITY-DRIVEN CRITERIA IN MIND[16]

In recent years, companies of all shapes and sizes have been shifting their paths by creating industry precedence through commendable acts of sustainability initiatives.

Chemical giant BASF went through a process that evaluated 50,000 product applications in the company's portfolio, representing sales of $64 billion. The analysis, which took almost two years to complete and involved 1,500 experts, resulted in more than a thousand specific plans for changing or phasing their products.

Similarly, CVS realized that selling cigarettes was inconsistent with its mission as a pharmacy to make people healthier. So the company decided to abandon an estimated $2 billion annually by discontinuing the sale of tobacco.

Another main brand, Panera Bread, announced its commitment to removing a "No No List" of over 150 ingredients from its menu to eliminate artificial colors, flavors, sweeteners, and preservatives.

These are just a few examples of brands trying to align their product lines along with a new sustainability strategy. These bold and risky steps taken by big brands show their willingness to be part of the great movement of sustainability.

INTENSIFYING COLLABORATION BETWEEN THE PEER TO PEER AND MAINSTREAM ECONOMIES[17]

This new concept invites big brands to take part in the peer-to-peer economy in many ways. For instance, GoodGym, a quickly growing group of UK runners, combines regular exercise with helping local communities – whether by visiting isolated elderly people or repairing various kinds of infrastructure. This peer-to-peer model has recently found another way to create even more shared value by partnering with mainstream footwear brand New Balance.

A GROWING ECO-SYSTEM OF PLAYERS AND INITIATIVES AROUND A CIRCULAR BUSINESS MODEL

"Circular economy" is a generic term for an industrial economy that is, by design or intention, restorative, and in which material flows are of two types, biological nutrients, designed to reenter the biosphere safely, and technical nutrients, which are unsuitable for the biosphere, like metals and most plastics.

The Closed Loop Fund, an ambitious consortium of major brands, has created a $100 million fund aimed at providing municipalities access to zero- and low-interest loans to build comprehensive recycling programs.

CHAPTER THIRTEEN

BRINGING SUSTAINABILITY AND MARKETING CLOSER

*"More and more companies are reaching out to their suppliers
and contractors to work jointly on issues of sustainability,
environmental responsibility, ethics, and compliance."*

—Simon Mainwaring

By this time, there should be little doubt in the minds of people about the possibility of sustainability becoming the master key for many of the inventions that the human race is yet to witness in the future.

As mentioned again and again, the key challenge that businesses face is finding the way to bring together the concepts of sustainability and marketing to obtain a desired result.

There are indeed many who still believe that a sustainable product does not have a long lifespan like other conventional products on the market.

They cite lack of good marketing initiative for their thoughts.

Hence, it is crucial to take concrete steps to align sustainability and marketing together to create a world that we can proudly gift to our future generations. In this chapter, we will go through a few of the forces that provide us with the promise that our dream will be a reality in the near future.

HOLONOMIC THINKING[18]

In their book, *Holonomics: Business Where People and Planet Matter,* Simon Robinson and Maria Moraes Robinson describe a new way of thinking, teaching business leaders how to adapt in innovative ways. It mentions four ways to fully understand the world, nature, people, and phenomena. They are:

- Thinking

- Feeling

- Sensing

- Intuition

The book also emphasizes human values like peace, love, truth, right-action, and non-violence as an integral part of any organization.

In other words, it encourages us to think holonomically rather than mechanically, and aims to bring together life-cycle analysis, systems thinking, spirituality, nature's interconnectedness, philosophy, literacy, physics, biology, and business together. It helps a reader to open his or her eyes to uncommon dimensions of thought that also have practical applications.

The book helps you understand the entire concept by dividing the content into three easy-to-follow parts:

- Dynamics of seeing

- Dynamics of nature

- Dynamics of business

In Part One, the authors concentrate on attempting to point out how mechanistic thinking in science can limit the mode of thinking and knowing in all other fields of human endeavor, a limitation rooted in the "ways of seeing" that are currently dominant in most societies.

In Part Two, the authors give a variety of examples from natural systems and emphasize the importance of seeing an organization as a whole. To drive home the point, they use the example of social insects, such as ants and termites. Though while being observed, an insect's individual actions may seem chaotic and disorganized. However, when studied collectively, insects' behavior can be viewed in a different light, and their extraordinary achievements appreciated. Similarly, holonomic thinking encourages the understanding of relationships in their wholeness.

Part Three is based on the words of Sergio Chaia, former president of Nextel Brazil, who argues that the ideal organization does not exist because everything is being transformed and is always evolving, whether genetically or energetically.

RESEARCH STUDIES CHARTING NEW TERRITORIES OF INTELLIGENCE[19]

This research refers to the studies that focus on acquiring fresh insights around the public's reactions to the sharing economy, circular business models, and net positive models by Wolff Olins, Salt, Dragon Rouge, and Forum for the Future.

Studies are also happening across the globe to understand the marketing strategies adopted by the leading consumer goods which include online communication strategy. For instance, a study by Matthew Yeomans considers the online communication strategies of the 17 fastest-moving consumer goods multinationals and 162 of their best-performing and most important individual brands, boasting 586 million Facebook fans in total.

CIRCULAR ECONOMY[20]

"Circular economy" is a generic term for an industrial economy that is, by design or intention, restorative and in which material flows are of two types:

• Biological nutrients, designed to re-enter the biosphere safely, and

• Technical nutrients, which are designed to circulate at high quality without entering the biosphere.

This is a departure from the linear model of economy which advocates "Take, Make, Dispose."

The circular economy believes in the idea of "cradle to cradle" (C2C). In other words, the focus is on industrial sustainability.

The main founding principles of this model are:

• Waste does not exist – This implies that no material can be considered as waste. Biological nutrients are non-toxic and can be simply composted. Technical nutrients—polymers, alloys and other man-made materials—are designed to be reused with minimal energy.

• Diversity is strength – While working towards the circular economy, we should focus on longer-lasting products, developed for upgrade, aging, and repair by considering strategies like emotionally-durable design. Diverse products, materials, and systems with many connections and scales are more resilient in the face of external shocks, than systems built simply for efficiency. Additionally, energy must come from renewable sources.

• System thinking – This implies the ability to understand how things influence one another within a whole.

The European Commission is aiming to present a new, more ambitious circular economy strategy to transform Europe into a more competitive resource-efficient economy, addressing a range of economic sectors, including waste.[21]

Similarly, Desso, the global carpets, carpet tiles, and sports pitches company, has tied up with Healthy Seas, a Journey from Waste to Wear which is a multi-industry initiative aimed at removing marine waste—particularly fishing nets—to create healthier seas. Desso turns the recycled marine litter into ECONYL® yarn for use in new carpets. The company also claims that over 90 percent of its commercial carpet tile collection is Cradle to Cradle® (C2C) certified, and over 50 percent of its carpet tiles contain ECONYL® yarn.

Compelling story-telling and authentic story-doing

How many of our actions and choices have been influenced by stories that we have heard? Brands need to build a story through their actions. According to Ty Montague, author of *True Story: How to Combine Story and Action to Transform Your Business*, people don't buy products; they take actions that help advance their own personal meta-story, and sometimes buying and using your product is one of those actions.

There has been a huge rise in the number of brands that find a considerable place in the market. In fact, it has risen from 2.5 million in 1997 to 10 million in 2011. With the change in advertising ways, it is no longer enough for these brands to declare their mission or values in a splashy ad.

Today's world demands story-doing, which includes the following elements as its foundation:

- The participants (your customers, partners, and employees)

- The protagonist (your company today)

- The stage (the world around your business)

- The quest (your driving ambition and contribution to the world) and your action map (the actions that will make your story real for participants)

Well-targeted employee engagements[22]

I would like to explain this concept through an example. Matter to a Million is a five-year global partnership between HP and nonprofit micro-lending platform Kiva.

Together, HP and Kiva have been able to achieve more than 100,000 HP employees lending over $4.2 million, in $25 increments, to intriguing entrepreneurs from a variety of backgrounds all over the world.

Matter to a Million found success in striking a chord with HP's global employee base by providing an easy, entertaining, and rewarding way to invest in meaningful projects. And this is just the beginning, with four and a half years of the program yet to unfold.

Purpose-aligned set of corporate values

In 2013, for the first time, 150 senior managers at Barclay's had an element of their compensation linked to what the company leadership refers to as the "five Cs"—customers, colleagues, citizenship, conduct, and company.

Starting in 2016, these five Cs are taken into account when evaluating the performance of all 140,000 employees globally.

The same should be the case with every brand in the world with a new, purpose-aligned set of corporate values being adopted by brands of all sizes and industries.

Building movements for behavior change at scale

As I have said before, it is not enough to send across the message of the company through flashy ads. Ad campaigns like Project Wild Thing, Good Gym, and Project Everyone are encouraging children and adults alike to go and frolic outdoors, get exercise, and enjoy our Mother Earth.

Good Gym, which gets people to exercise while running errands for lonely elderly folks, is spreading fast around the UK, and Project Everyone aims to put the revised 2015 UN Sustainable Development

Goals into the hands of roughly seven billion people in seven days next fall. A generation of movement makers are afoot, and they aim to make a difference, aligning change with collective consciousness and individual desire for change.

CHAPTER FOURTEEN

TOP GREEN MARKETING CAMPAIGNS

"I think if the people who work for a business are proud of the business they work for, they'll work that much harder, and therefore, I think turning your business into a real force for good is good business sense, as well."

—Richard Branson, Virgin Group

Over the years, we have witnessed several successful marketing campaigns around the world, targeting different audiences. There is no doubt that spreading awareness about the concept of sustainability is one of the major ways to find success in a commodity market. Here is a list of the most successful green marketing campaigns to date.

THE TIDE COLDWATER CHALLENGE[23]

In 2005, Proctor & Gamble joined hands with Save Energy to launch a consumer education campaign that aimed at convincing households to begin washing clothes in chilly water.

According to P&G estimates, only 38 percent of laundry loads globally are washed in cool water. This campaign successfully attempted to break the myth that clothes are best washed in warm water, thereby saving a lot of energy consumption in a household.

The campaign encouraged people to wash their laundry sustainably by washing at lower temperatures, knowing that Tide Coldwater Clean is specially formulated to work effectively in cold water for outstanding stain removal and brilliant color protection.

The company also set a corporate sustainability goal of converting 70 percent of total global washing machine loads to cold water washing by 2020. As part of the initiative, the company invested in cleaner technology and business innovation, developing solutions to enable economic growth while avoiding emissions and reducing water consumption, committing to reduce the environmental impact in our own operations, and developing strategic partnerships.

GE Ecomagination

Nearly 8,000 Power & Water employees have joined the Ecomagination Nation, committing to personally helping decrease GE's carbon footprint, energy, and water consumption to solve some of the toughest environmental challenges at scale to create a cleaner, faster, smarter tomorrow.

Jamie Oliver and the Feed Me Better campaign[24]

Jamie Oliver, the outspoken English chef, started his Feed Me Better campaign in 2005, appalled by the junk food being served at many schools in England. He started 'Jamie's School Dinners' program on Channel 4, where he initially struggled to persuade children to try dishes other than chips, burgers, and some other unhealthy foods.

The campaign attracted 271,677 signatures of support for Oliver's petition to improve the state of school meals, which was duly handed over to Downing Street. The first step was to replace the Turkey Twizzler and chips with salads and fruit. He used disruptive media and public visibility to communicate and motivate, creating a new kind of million that would contribute to helping all schools across England provide healthier, more nutritional meals. In February 2010, Oliver was awarded the 2009 TED Prize for his campaigns to create change on both the individual and governmental levels.

TOM SHOES & PROJECT HOLIDAY[25]

During the Christmas season in 2008, Blake Mycosky, creator and founder of TOM Shoes, launched the campaign to sell 30,000 shoes so that they could send the same number of shoes to children in Ethiopia who are fighting against a completely preventable disease called podoconiosis. They get this disease from walking in silica – rich, ancient volcanic mud – without shoes. Simply wearing shoes prevents this disease entirely.

The campaign was very simple: buy a pair, get a pair. Eminent personalities like Bill Clinton and Anna Wintour gave their support to the campaign. The company exceeded its goal by 23 percent and raised unprecedented awareness for its cause, all without paid media.

Timberland and Earthkeeper's Campaign

In 2008, The Timberland Company launched a new marketing campaign, Earthkeeper, with a goal of recruiting one million people to become part of an online network designed to inspire environmental change. They also unveiled a new Earthkeeper's product collection along with it, which included Timberland's modern, stylish, and eco-conscious Fall 2009 footwear collections.

The campaign consisted of TV, print, and online work, and supported Earthkeepers' apparel, which was established to demonstrate the company's environmental values. It included retail promotions, online social network tools, and company service days where Timberland employees engaged with green products in their local area. Online activity through interactive games and banner ads also supported the campaign.

The countries in focus were U.S., Italy, and the U.K. For this purpose, the company partnered with UK-based creative agency Leagas Delaney to create a bold, new "Bait" advertising campaign to support Timberland Mountain Athletics, the company's new line of environmentally-conscious, multi-sport outdoor shoes for young adventurers in and around cities.

HSBC AND THE THERE IS NO SMALL CHANGE CAMPAIGN

They started their campaign in Florida, California, Connecticut, New York, and New Jersey and had radio, print, online, and outdoor ad components, along with a three-month calendar of earth-friendly events listed on their microsite.

A Green Living Kit, including green coupons, a subscription to The Green Guide from National Geographic, and other giveaways were sent to each new checking or business checking customer who opted to pay at least three bills online.

WWF AND THE #LASTSELFIE CAMPAIGN

The WWF brand researched behavior on different social channels (including how Snapchat users shared content, as well as what types of image were being saved as a screenshot) in an attempt to better understand users and establish long-term relationships with them. The campaign used Snapchat's native timed message functionality to convey the idea that time was running out for endangered species.

Users who follow WWF on Snapchat receive a #LastSelfie—an image of an endangered animal—with a message stating it could be the last time the user sees it. Snapchat users who receive an image they'd like to keep for longer than nine seconds can use their phone's screenshot function to permanently save it, and share it on social media such as Twitter.

Encouraging users to screenshot and share WWF's images was vital to the campaign's success, so the brand teamed with social influencers to help start the trend.

Beyond Meat and Plant-Based Burgers

The biggest problem facing our generation is climate change. And one of the biggest contributors to this environmental crisis?

The meat industry.

There's no denying that meat production is having significantly adverse effects on our environment. Beyond Meat is shaking up the food industry by creating delicious, plant-based "meat" products that are better for human health, the environment, climate change and animals. Beyond Meat's branding focuses on the good they're doing for the environment and their consumers.

CHAPTER FIFTEEN

CONCLUDING THOUGHTS

"If you want creativity, take off one zero. If you want sustainability, take off two zeros."

—Jaime Lerner

As consumers, we should know how to identify brands and products that have a sustainable life cycle. In our journey towards creating a sustainable planet, there are many things that we need to care about. Most importantly, we need to realize our choices are not just going to impact the lifespan of the planet, but also the survival of our future generations.

As consumers of a vast range of products, we need to figure out what's cruel and what's kind. It is through our acceptance of such products that we can encourage and push for more green products and through them a healthier lifestyle.

All this is only possible if we are aware of ways to choose the correct product. We can now understand that educating the citizens of the issues surrounding the survival is the only true path.

SOURCES

1. Bach, V. (2013). New ISO 18600 Series released on Packaging and the environment - Includes ISO 18601, ISO 18602, ISO 18603, ISO 18604, ISO 18605 and ISO 18606 - Document Center's Standards Forum. Document Center's Standards Forum. Retrieved 30 June 2015, from http://standardsforum.com/new-iso-18600-series-released-on-packaging-and-the-environment-includes-iso-18601-iso-18602-iso-18603-iso-18604-iso-18605-and-iso-18606/

2. Designrecycleinc.com. (2015). Compare: LED Lights vs CFL vs Incandescent Lighting Chart. Retrieved 30 June 2015, from http://www.designrecycleinc.com/led%20comp%20chart.html

3. Desso. (2015). Cradle to Cradle® carpet company Desso launches new circular economy material stream of up to 20,000 tons of chalk from local water companies. Retrieved 7 August 2015, from http://www.desso.com/news-events/news-overview/2014/11/cradle-to-cradler-carpet-company-desso-launches-new-circular-economy-material-stream-of-up-to-20000-tonnes-of-chalk-from-local-water-companies/

4. Ec.europa.eu. (2015). Moving towards a circular economy - Environment - European Commission. Retrieved 7 August 2015, from http://ec.europa.eu/environment/circular-economy/index_en.htm

5. Ec.europa.eu. (2015). Packaging and packaging waste - European Commission. Retrieved 30 June 2015, from http://ec.europa.eu/growth/single-market/european-standards/harmonised-standards/packaging/index_en.htm

6. Echa.europa.eu. (2015). REACH - ECHA. Retrieved 30 June 2015, from http://echa.europa.eu/regulations/reach

7. Epa.gov. (2015). List of Greener Products Programs | Greener Products | US EPA. Retrieved 7 August 2015, from http://www.epa.gov/greenerproducts/programs/

8. Fda.gov, (2015). Prohibited & Restricted Ingredients. Retrieved 30 June 2015, from http://www.fda.gov/Cosmetics/

GuidanceRegulation/LawsRegulations/ucm127406.htm#prohibited

9. Feedmebetter.com. (2015). Feed me better. Retrieved 7 August 2015, from http://www.feedmebetter.com/

10. Footprintnetwork.org. (2015). Footprint Basics - Overview. Retrieved 30 June 2015, from http://www.footprintnetwork.org/en/index.php/GFN/page/footprint_basics_overview/

11. Ftc.gov, (2015). Fair Packaging and Labeling Act | Federal Trade Commission. Retrieved 30 June 2015, from https://www.ftc.gov/enforcement/rules/rulemaking-regulatory-reform-proceedings/fair-packaging-labeling-act

12. Gdrc.org, (2015). Life Cycle Assessment. Retrieved 30 June 2015, from http://www.gdrc.org/uem/lca/lca-define.html

13. Gdrc.org, (2015). Sustainability Concepts: Natural Step. Retrieved 30 June 2015, from http://www.gdrc.org/sustdev/concepts/19-n-step.html

14. Gdrc.org, (2015). Waste Management: Fact Sheet. Retrieved 30 June 2015, from http://www.gdrc.org/uem/waste/waste-factsheet.html

15. Ghimire, S., Johnston, J., Ingression, W., & Hawkins, T. (2014). Life Cycle Assessment of Domestic and Agricultural Rainwater Harvesting Systems. Environmental Science & Technology, 48(7), 4069-4077. doi:10.1021/es500189f

16. Horowitz, B. (2008). So, You Think You Have Nothing to Wear: TOMS Project Holiday-Give 30,000 Pairs of Shoes in 30 days. Barbrahorowitz.blogspot.in. Retrieved 7 August 2015, from http://barbrahorowitz.blogspot.in/2008/12/toms-project-holiday.html

17. http://www.ecocycle.org/, (2010). Facts and Figures to Inspire Action toward Zero Waste. Retrieved 30 June 2015, from http://www.ecocycle.org/files/pdfs/Eco-CycleEnvironmentalFacts.pdf

18. James, Z. (2015). Salt | Five Celebrities Who Stand for Sustainability. Salt. Retrieved 7 August 2015, from http://www.wearesalt.org/five-celebrities-who-stand-for-sustainability/

19. News.pg.com, (2015). Tide® Challenges Americans to Switch to Cold Water During Earth Week | P&G News | Events, Multimedia, Public Relations. Retrieved 7 August 2015, from http://news.pg.com/press-release/pg-corporate-announcements/tide-challenges-americans-switch-cold-water-during-earth-we

20. Nuke Suite, (2015). 3 Game-Changing Case Studies in Green Marketing. Retrieved 7 August 2015, from https://www.nukesuite.com/green-marketing-social-media-campaign/

21. Oecd.org, (2015). Extended Producer Responsibility - OECD. Retrieved 30 June 2015, from http://www.oecd.org/env/tools-evaluation/extendedproducerresponsibility.htm

22. Rainforest-alliance.org, (2015). Follow the Frog 2015-2016 | Rainforest Alliance. Retrieved 7 August 2015, from http://www.rainforest-alliance.org/marketing/followthefrog

23. sustainablebrands.com, (2015). 10 Critical Corporate Sustainability Trends to Watch in 2015 and Beyond | Sustainable Brands. Retrieved 7 August 2015, from http://www.sustainablebrands.com/news_and_views/blog/dimitar_vlahov/10_critical_corporate_sustainability_trends_watch_2015_beyond

24. sustainablebrands.com, (2015). 10 Forces That Are Bringing Sustainability and Marketing Closer Together (Finally!) | Sustainable Brands. Retrieved 7 August 2015, from http://www.sustainablebrands.com/news_and_views/blog/dimitar_vlahov/10_forces_are_bringing_sustainability_marketing_closer_together_f

25. sustainablebrands.com, (2015). What Is Holonomic Thinking and Why Should You Care? | Sustainable Brands. Retrieved 7 August 2015, from http://www.sustainablebrands.com/news_and_views/stakeholder_trends_insights/tamay_kiper/what_holonomic_thinking_why_should_you_care

26. TerraChoice Environmental Marketing Inc. (2009).

27. The Three Levels of Sustainability. (2012). Management of Env Quality, 23(4). doi:10.1108/meq.2012.08323daa.010

28. The Water Project. (2015). Statistics. Retrieved 30 June 2015,

from http://thewaterproject2o.weebly.com/statistics.html

29. Unep.org. (2015). resource-efficiency > Business > Sustainable Products > Design for Sustainability. Retrieved 30 June 2015, from http://www.unep.org/resourceefficiency/Business/SustainableProducts/DesignforSustainability/tabid/78845/Default.aspx

30. Water.epa.gov. (2015). Regulatory Information | Regulatory Information | US EPA. Retrieved 30 June 2015, from http://water.epa.gov/lawsregs/rulesregs/

31. Yale School of Forestry & Environmental Studies. (2015). Retrieved from http://environment.yale.edu/climate-communication/files/GfK%2oRoper%2oYale%2oSurvey%2o-%2o Summer%2o2oo8%2oFINAL.pdf

ENDNOTES

1. The Three Levels of Sustainability. (2012). Management of Env Quality, 23(4). doi:10.1108/meq.2012.08323daa.010

2. Gdrc.org, (2015). Sustainability Concepts: Natural Step. Retrieved 30 June 2015, from http://www.gdrc.org/sustdev/concepts/19-n-step.html

3. Footprintnetwork.org, (2015). Footprint Basics - Overview. Retrieved 30 June 2015, from

4. http://www.ecocycle.org/, (2010). Facts and Figures to Inspire Action toward Zero Waste. Retrieved 30 June 2015.

5. Gdrc.org, (2015). Waste Management: Fact Sheet. Retrieved 30 June 2015, from http://www.gdrc.org/uem/waste/waste-factsheet.html

6. Gdrc.org. (2015). Life Cycle Assessment. Retrieved 30 June 2015, from http://www.gdrc.org/uem/lca/lca-define.html

7. The Water Project. (2015). Statistics. Retrieved 30 June 2015, from http://thewaterprojecth2o.weebly.com/statistics.html

8. Fda.gov. (2015). Prohibited & Restricted Ingredients. Retrieved 30 June 2015, from http://www.fda.gov/Cosmetics/GuianceRegulation/LawsRegulations/ucm127406.htm#prohibited

9. Source: GfK Roper Public Affairs & Media and the Yale School of Forestry & Environmental Studies Survey on Environmental Issues (2008)

10. TerraChoice Environmental Marketing Inc. (2009).

11. Bach, V. (2013). New ISO 18600 Series released on Packaging and the environment - Includes ISO 18601, ISO 18602, ISO 18603, ISO 18604, ISO 18605 and ISO 18606- Document Center's Standards Forum/

12. Eceuropa.eu. (2015). Packaging and packaging waste -

European Commission. Retrieved 30 June 2015, from http://ec.europa.eu/growth/single-market/european-standards/harmonised-standards/packaging/index_en.htm

13. Epa.gov. (2015). List of Greener Products Programs | Greener Products | US EPA. Retrieved 7 August 2015, from http://www.epa.gov/greenerproducts/programs/

14. James, Z. (2015). Salt | Five Celebrities Who Stand for Sustainability. Salt. from http://www.wearesalt.org/five-celebrities-who-stand-for-sustainability/

15. Rainforest-alliance.org. (2015). Follow the Frog 2015-2016 | Rainforest Alliance. Retrieved 7 August 2015, from http://www.rainforest-alliance.org/marketing/followthefrog

16. Sustainablebrands.com. (2015). 10 Critical Corporate Sustainability Trends to Watch in 2015 and Beyond | Sustainable Brands. Retrieved 7 August 2015, from http://www.sustainablebrands.com/news_and_views/blog/dimitar_vlahov/10_critical_corporate_sustainability_trends_watch_2015_beyond

17. sustainablebrands.com. (2015). 10 Critical Corporate Sustainability Trends to Watch in 2015 and Beyond | Sustainable Brands. Retrieved 7 August 2015, from http://www.sustainablebrands.com/news_and_views/blog/dimitar_vlahov/10_critical_corporate_sustainability_trends_watch_2015_beyond

18. sustainablebrands.com. (2015). What Is Holonomic Thinking and Why Should You Care? | Sustainable Brands. Retrieved 7 August 2015, from http://www.sustainablebrands.com/news_and_views/stakeholder_trends_insights/tamay_kiper/what_holonomic_thinking_why_should_you_care

19. sustainablebrands.com. (2015). 10 Forces That Are Bringing Sustainability and Marketing Closer Together (Finally!) | Sustainable Brands. Retrieved 7 August 2015, from http://www.sustainablebrands.com/news_and_views/blog/dimitar_vlahov/10_forces_are_bringing_sustainability_marketing_closer_together_f

20. Ec.europa.eu. (2015). Moving towards a circular economy -

Environment - European Commission. Retrieved 7 August 2015, from http://ec.europa.eu/environment/circular-economy/index_en.htm

21. Desso. (2015). Cradle to Cradle® carpet company Desso launches new circular economy material stream of up to 20,000 tons of chalk from local water companies. Retrieved 7 August 2015, from http://www.desso.com/news-events/news-overview/2014/11/cradle-to-cradler-carpet-company-desso-launches-new-circular-economy-material-stream-of-up-to-20000-tonnes-of-chalk-from-local-water-companies/

22. Desso. (2015). Cradle to Cradle® carpet company Desso launches new circular economy material stream of up to 20,000 tons of chalk from local water companies. Retrieved 7 August 2015, from http://www.desso.com/news-events/news-overview/2014/11/cradle-to-cradler-carpet-company-desso-launches-new-circular-economy-material-stream-of-up-to-20000-tonnes-of-chalk-from-local-water-companies/

23. News.pg.com. (2015). Tide® Challenges Americans to Switch to Cold Water During Earth Week | P&G News | Events, Multimedia, Public Relations. Retrieved 7 August 2015, from http://news.pg.com/press-release/pg-corporate-announcements/tide-challenges-americans-switch-cold-water-during-earth-we

24. Feedmebetter.com. (2015). Feed me better. Retrieved 7 August 2015, from http://www.feedmebetter.com/

25. Horowitz, B. (2008). So You Think You Have Nothing to Wear: TOMS Project Holiday-Give 30,000 pairs of shoes in 30 days. Barbrahorowitz.blogspot.in. Retrieved 7 August 2015, from http://barbrahorowitz.blogspot.in/2008/12/toms-project-holiday.html

PROFESSIONAL ACKNOWLEDGMENTS

CHRYSALIS PUBLISHING AUTHOR SERVICES
www.chrysalis-pub.com
chrysalispub@gmail.com

Made in the USA
Middletown, DE
08 September 2018